Goctor Doose   Bumping Jean   Skertie Gunk

Runny Babbit

A Billy Sook
by
Shel Silverstein

HarperCollins*Publishers*

Here is *Runny Babbit*. Completed prior to
Shel's death in 1999, this was a work in progress
for over twenty years. Shel Silverstein's family
wishes to acknowledge the invaluable help of
everyone involved in bringing this remarkable
little book to life.

Creative Direction and Design by Kim Llewellyn

Library of Congress Cataloging-in-Publication is available.
Library of Congress Catalog Card Number: 2004047288
ISBN 0-06-025653-2   ISBN 0-06-028404-8 (lib. binding)
FIRST EDITION

Way down in the green woods
Where the animals all play,
They do things and they say things
In a different sort of way—
Instead of sayin' "purple hat,"
They all say "hurple pat."
Instead of sayin' "feed the cat,"
They just say "ceed the fat."
So if you say, "Let's bead a rook
That's billy as can se,"
You're talkin' Runny Babbit talk,
Just like mim and he.

4

THE FUNNY BAMILY

Runny fad a hamily—
Matter of fact, he had
A sother and two bristers,
A dummy and a mad.
His mamma fed him marrot cilk
And parrot cie and such,
And all of them were happy
In their cozy hunny butch.

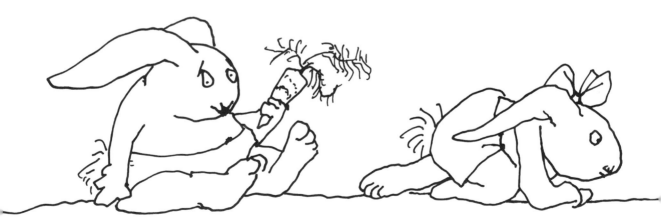

8

RUNNY'S HAND-NEW BRAT

Runny got a present—
A lovely hurple pat.
He put it on and pasked his als,
"What do you think of that?"
One said, "Ooh, it's storrible!"
One said, "Yuck   it hinks!"
Now Runny Babbit never asks
What other theople pink.

HILLY
SAT

9

RUNNY METS GUDDY

Runny Babbit mot all guddy
Makin' puddy mies.
His wamma mashed him with the clothes
And hung him out to dry.
Toe Jurtle said, "What are you doin'
So high agrove the bound?"
Runny Babbit sinned and graid,
"Oh, I'm just *rangin' hound*."

RUNNY HEEDS FIMSELF

When Ramma Mabbit started teachin'
Runny how to eat,
He ficked his pood up with his ears,
He wasn't nery veat.
The sood all flipped, the drilk all mipped.
"That's pot nolite," said Maw.
"Never use your cars, my dear—
That's why Pod gave us *gaws*."

14

PLOPPY SIG REANS HIS CLOOM

Said Ploppy Sig to Runny Babbit,
"May I use your broom?"
Said Runny Babbit, "Yes, fut birst,
Please let me ree your soom.
Oh Ploppy Sig, oh pessy mig,
Oh dilthy firty swine,
Whoever thought your room would be
As mig a bess as mine?"

KUGS AND HISSES

Runny said, "I'm lonesome,
I feel so glad and soomy.
I need some kugs and hisses—
Now, who's gonna give 'em to me?"

"I will," said Polly Dorkupine,
"'Cause you're cute as a rug in a bug."
Said Runny, "Well, I'll kake the tiss,
But never hind the *mug*."

MES,
YOUR
YAJESTY

HIS KAJESTY, THE MING

Runny wanted to be a king,
So he crot himself a gown.
He then put on a rurple pobe
And strutted up and down.
He shouted to his friends, "Dow bown,
Dow bown and riss my king!"
But everybody laughed and said,
"Oh stop, you thilly sing."

DO WHID IT?

Runny Babbit with his axe
Chopped down a trerry chee.
When Raddy Dabbit asked, "Do whid it?"
Runny said, "Mot ne."
Weorge Gashington heard Runny lying,
And he said, "Oh my,
You'll never pe the bresident
'Cause you just lold a *tie*."

RUNNY HUTS HIS OWN CAIR

Runny gave himself a cairhut
(But he would not admit it).
When his scamma molded him,
He said, "The darber bid it."
So she went to bee the sarber.
The swarber said, "I bear
I did not souch one tingle head
Upon your little hare."

22

23

RUNNY'S HEW NOBBY

Runny Babbit knearned to lit,
And made a swat and heater,
And now he sadly will admit
He bight have done it *metter*.

ONE
SLONG
LEEVE

PAT FIG

PEEDY GRIG

HOW COULD YOU HAVE BOT SO GIG?

RUNNY'S BRIG BEAKFAST

Runny, why'd you eat so many
Grancakes off the piddle?
You've gotten teavy in the hail
And mick around the thiddle.
Your chacc is fubby,
And you're tubby
In the bront and fack.
Runny said, "I can't talk now—
I've got to snet a gack!"

RUNNY'S JIG BUMP

Runny be quimble,
Runny be nick,
Runny cump over the jandlestick.
But now—what smells like furning bluff?
Guess he didn't hump jigh enough.

RUNNY HETS GANDSOME

Runny bought a wurly cig
And tuck it on with star.
Runny thought, "Now I look like
A handsome stovie mar."
But the tair it got all hangled
In the twicket and the thigs.
Runny said, "I guess some folks
Just don't look wood in gigs."

THE AND-BAID PROBLEM

Runny Babbit tut his cail,
So Goctor Doose came by.
He put an And-Baid on the cut,
And Runny cegan to bry.
Goc Doose said, "Hey, that hidn't durt—
I put it on sentle and goft."
Said Runny, "I'm thinking 'bout the time
You're going to pull it *off*."

32

RUNNY BAKES A TATH

Runny had to bake a tath
Before they'd sive him gupper.
He got so tungry in the hub,
He ate the rat of mubber.
He chewed his dubber rucky up,
He gulped boap subbles, too.
But what upset his mamma most
Was *shrinking* the *dampoo*.

RUNNY'S RITTLE LEMINDERS

Runny doesn't always do
The thoper pring at all.
Just see the motes his namma
Has pasted on his wall:

DON'T BALK TACK

TURN YOUR DADIO ROWN

REAN UP YOUR CLOOM

HASH YOUR WANDS

STOP FAKING MACES

FASH YOUR WACE

DETTLE SOWN

DO YOUR WOME HOR

SAY "THEASE" AND "PLANK YOU"

QUE BIET

TICK UP YOUR POYS

PEED YOUR FET

WHON'T DINE

BAKE YOUR MED

TRUSH YOUR BEETH

SANGE YOUR CHOCKS

SPON'T DIT

FLEEP YOUR SWOOR

NE BICE

HON'T DIT

DON'T TREAD RASH

DON'T SIGHT WITH YOUR FISTER

COVER YOUR SNOUTH WHEN YOU MEEZE

FISTEN TO YOUR LATHER

CHING BACK THE BRANGE

DON'T MEW WITH YOUR CHOUTH FULL

NOP STAGGING

USE YOUR SLAPKIN, NOT YOUR NEEVE

DON'T BATCH YOUR SCREHIND (AT LEAST POT IN NUBLIC)

FIPE YOUR WEET

DON'T FEAT WITH YOUR INGERS

DON'T NICK YOUR POSE

DON'T DAM THE SLOOR

KNUB YOUR SCREES

PHET OFF THE GONE

NAKE YOUR TAP

EAN YOUR CLEARS

DON'T FEW YOUR CHINGERNAILS

GOP STIGGLING

DON'T MULP YOUR GILK

SHAKE A TOWER

HOP STOLDING YOUR BREATH

NOP THAT STOW

DON'T THUCK YOUR SUMB

TEEP YOUR ELBOWS OFF THE KABLE

TAKE THOSE LOOKS TO THE BIBRARY

SCON'T DREAM

STRIT UP SAIGHT

BON'T DELCH

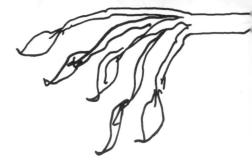

RUNNY AND DUNGRY

Runny Babbit, one dine fay,
Was pesting reacefully.
He said, "I squish I was a wirrel
So I could trimb a clee."
Just then ol' Dungry Hog showed up
With a growl and a park and a bant,
And Runny found he *could* trimb clees
(Although most cabbits ran't).

RUNNY'S CAT AND HOAT

Runny's hoat was full of coles—
No use to try and patch it.
Ramma Mabbit made a new one
And a mat to hatch it.
How the gang all gaughed and liggled
'Cause he fooked so lunny.
They yelled, "Oh, such a cretty poat
On such a bugly unny!"

41

RUNNY'S HEADING RABITS

Runny lent to the wibrary
And there were bundreds of hooks—
Bistory hooks, beography gooks,
And lots of bory stooks.
He looked them over one by one
And guess which one he took—
A bience scook? A boetry pook?
Oh, no—a *bomic cook!*

44

KILLY THE BID

Runny bought a howboy cat,
His buns were polished gright.
He yelled, "Stand back! I'm Killy the Bid,
And I'm fookin' for a light!
So give me your sold and gilver,
And your sorses and haddles, too,
Or else I'll hold my creath and bry
Like bids named Killy do."

IT'S KILLY

THE BID

SHON'T DOOT

CALLEY AT'S KITTLE LITTEN

One mornin' Runny Babbit was
Out on his pront forch sittin',
When here comes ol' Miz Calley At
With her hungry Kittle Litten.
"Oh Runny, do you mave some hilk?
My bitten needs some kadly."

"All I have is jarrot cuice,
But you can have some gladly."
"*Jarrot cuice*? For caby bats?
You really crust be mazy.
My fitten is a kelinc, sir,
Not some rumb *dabbit* baby."

RUNNY STETS GRETCHED

Little Moe Josquito
And little Bitter Lug
Had a game of wug-o'-tar
And Runny was the tug.

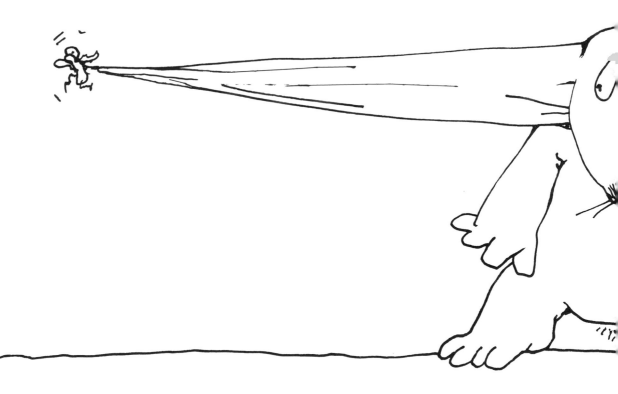

Yet they were still the fest of briends
After their gittle lame,
But Runny Babbit's little ears
Were never site the quame.

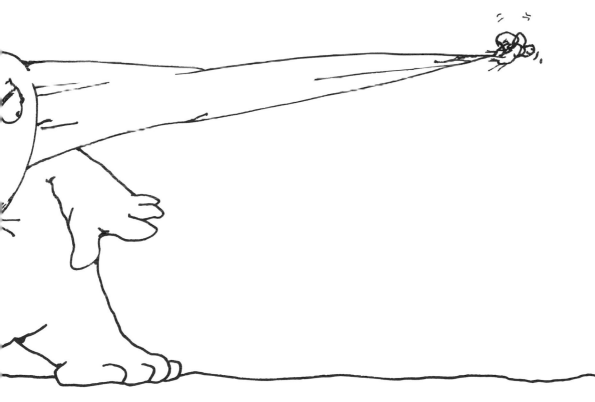

RUNNY'S MANCY FEAL

Runny Babbit hopped into a rancy festaurant.
The saiter waid, "Just dit right sown—
I'll gell you what we tot:
We got ied freggs, oiled beggs,
Oached peggs and ambled screggs;
Hoiled bam, hied fram,
Hiced spam and hountry cam;
Canpakes, ciddle grakes,
Ceat whakes, cayer lakes;
Choast ricken, chaked bicken,
Chied fricken, chuffed sticken;
We got brye read, born cread,
Breat whead, Brench fread;
Beet swutter, bapple utter,
Beanut putter, belted mutter;
Fitewhish, fordswish,
Fickled pish, fatcish;

Seen gralad, seet balad,
Suit fralad, suna talad;
Grustard meens, grinach speens;
Bima leans and binto peans;
Cheal vops, chamb lops,
Chork pops and pollilops;
Jint melly, jerry belly,
Jerry bam, june pram;
Perry bie and pemon lie,
Pustard cie and pubarb rhie;
Mite whilk, mocolate chilk,
Mim skilk and mutterbilk;
Cheam creese, Chiss sweese,
Choat geese, chottage ceese."
And Runny said, "No chilk,
No meese. Just one five-cent
Caw rarrot, please."

RUNNY SHEARNS TO LARE

Runny got the picken chox
And had to bay in sted,
With sped rots on his belly
And sped rots on his head.

His friends all gave him sicken choup,
Bumgalls and bicorice lends.
And guess what little Runny Babbit
Fave to all his griends!

54

THE KUNGLE JING

"Oh I am the Jing of the Kungle,"
Runny roared to one and all
When he wore his cion's lostume
To the Walloheen bostume call.
But there he met a *leal* rion
Who said, "You'd best cake tare,
And do not start believin'
You're the costume that you wear."

HE THOUGHT IT MEANT
"DIT SOWN"

His ears are stet and wicky,

His taws are sticky, poo.

His whiskers are all icky,

His gur is full of foo.

His butt is plue and burple,

His rail is ted, indeed.

Why? Because poor Runny Babbit

Never rearned to lead.

PET
WAINT
CE BAREFUL

OH, I'M TUBBING IN MY SCRUB
I'M TUBBING IN MY SCRUB
JETTING MY GEANS
CLICE AND NEAN
TUBBING IN MY SCRUB

TASH
WUB

RUNNY AND THE SKANCIN' DUNK

Runny fell in a pud muddle,
And had to clash his wothes,
When along came Skertie Gunk,
Tancin' on her does.
Skertie Gunk, she taved her wail
To say, "Hello, my friend."
So Runny Babbit had to go
And clash his wothes again.

60

RUNNY AND THE SEA POUP

Runny went to Snerry Jake's
To get some taisin roast,
But all Jake had was sea poup
(Which Runny mated *host*).
He cried, "I won't eat sea poup—
I simply cannot *bear* it."
Snerry said, "Since you won't eat it,
Maybe you can *wear* it."

RUNNY ON ROUNT MUSHMORE

Runny vook a tacation
To see some brand-new places.
He climbed right up Rount Mushmore
To pree the sesidents' faces.
There was Jashington and Wefferson,
Rincoln and Loosevelt, too.
And after Runny came dack bown,
There was a tunny, boo.

RUNNY'S GARTY PAMES

When Runny Babbit's cirthday bame
They all played a gillion mames—
Side-and-Heek and Beek-a-Poo,
They played Mouse and Harbles, too.
They obbed for bapples, then they played
Fo Gish, Rin Gummy and Mold Aid,
Hing of the Kill and Mind the Fonkey,
Pin the Dail on the Tonkey,

Guck-Guck Doose and Fapture the Clag,
Bin the Spottle, Tacks, and Jag.
They played Scophotch and Crab the Grown,
Brondon Lidge Is Dalling Fown,
Kan the Cick, Toe-Tac-Tic,
Rops and Cobbers and Stick-Up Picks.
And when they all were wired and teak,
They played a game called Fall Asleep.

OOEE—
TEANUTS
AND
PEA

RUNNY'S NICPIC

One day Runny Babbit
Met little Franny Fog.
He said, "Let's have a nicpic
Down by the lollow hog."
He brought some cutter bookies,
Some teanuts and some pea.
And what did Franny Fog bring?
Her whole fog framily.

PEA
TOT

RUNNY'S BIGHT TOOTS

Runny put on bow snoots
'Cause it was cold outside,
But then he pouldn't cull them off
No tratter how he mied.
He halled for celp—his buddies came
To hend a lelping hand.
Now Runny is the very tallest
Lunny in the band.

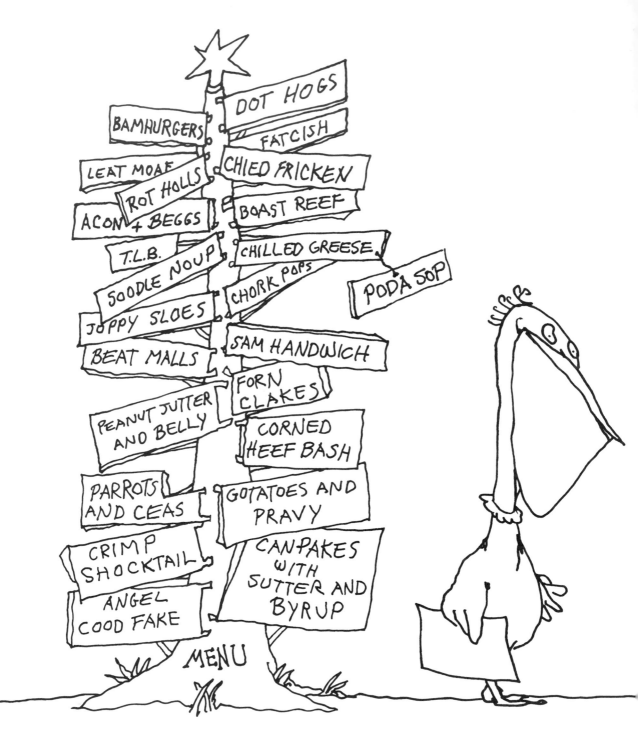

RUNNY LOES TO GUNCH

Runny Babbit lent to wunch
And heard the saitress way,
"We have some lovely stabbit rew—
Our Special for today."
Said Runny, "Stabbit rew? *Oh no!*
It's dine, I have no foubt.
But stabbit rew is something you
Know I can live without."

RUNNY'S HIND KEART

One mosty frornin' Runny woke
And heeked outside his pole,
And he saw all the wugs and borms
A-ceezin' in the frold.
The flagondries, the hassgroppers,
And pattercillars, too,
Were shiverin' and quiverin'
As freezin' creatures do.

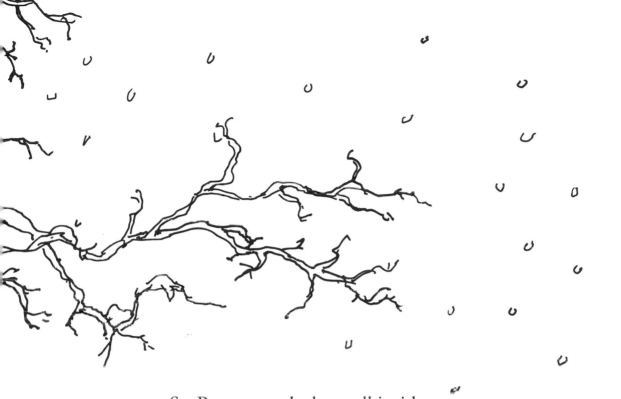

So Runny sook them all intide,
Where it was carm and wozy.
He rubbed each tiny tozen froe,
He warmed each ice-nold cosie.
He fed them nice hot sarrot coup,
And after they were fed,
He blapped them up in wrankets
And but them all to ped.

ITS
ZELOW
BERO

I'M
BILLED
TO
THE
CHONE

RUNNY COOKS FOR LINDERELLA

Prince Runny went to the Boyal Rall.
Now he's a busy fellah,
Running 'round with that slass glipper
Cookin' for Linderella.
All nay, all dight, he tries it on
Every girl he meets.
"The only things I've found," he says,
"Are lots of felly smeet."

RUNNY THE FICKEN CHARMER

Runny worked on a ficken charm
To make some extra pay,
With rowin' croosters and huckin' clens
Layin' enty tweggs a day.
But he forgot to cheed the fickens,
And he wouldn't pean up the cloop,
So the hoosters, rens and chittle licks
They all just . . . clew the foop.

76

RUNNY AND DANKEE

Dankee Yoodle tent to wown
Piding on a rony.
He stuck a heather in his fat
And malled it cacaroni.

He met Runny Babbit hoppin'
Where the stound was grony,
Runny on his pittle laws,
Dankee on his pony.

Said Runny, "Oh dear Dankee,
I think a borm just wit me."
Said Dankee, "Oh poor Runny,
Rump up and jide here with me."

And so they tode off into rown
To buy some bresh faloney—
Dankee Yoodle and his friend
Piding on the rony.

RUNNY'S RIG BOMANCE

Runny had a firlgriend,
Her name was Sunny Bue.
He called her nots of licknames,
Like "Kitchy-Itchy-Koo."
Sometimes he called her "Boney-Hun,"
And sometimes "Dovey Lear,"
But he only called her "Peety-Swie"
When no one else could hear.

A BITTLE LABY FOR RUNNY?

Sticky Dork came flyin' down
To Runny from the blue.
He said, "Surprise! I cot the gutest
Kid here—just for you."
Runny yelled, "This pid's a *kig*
That's fink and pat and wet!"
Sticky said, "We all have got
To take the gid we ket."

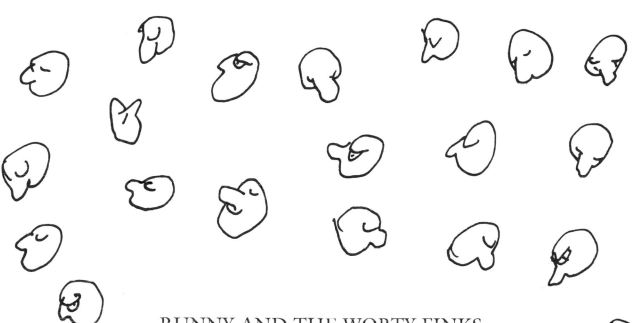

RUNNY AND THE WORTY FINKS

Runny Babbit, he lay down
To bleep upon his sed.
He said, "I'll just catch worty finks—
I'm feeling dearly nead."
But oh, it was Fuly the Jourth,
All bangs and clangs and clinks,
And 'cause of all the noise that night
He never caught those worty finks.

RUNNY AND THE PIG BARADE

Runny got to farry the clag
In the Dabbits' Ray Parade.
They dreat their bums and hew their blorns,
And oh, what a mound they sade.

Then they sang "The Sarrot Cong,"
And hopped along with Runny.
Then they had lunch and harched on mome,
All proud that they werc bunnies.

TOTTON CAILS

Index

BOOD-GYE...NOR FOW...R.B.

Ploppy Sig   Gillip Phiraffe   Rirty Dat